Why Is This Festival Special?

Divali

Jillian Powell

A⁺
Smart Apple Media

First published in 2005 by Franklin Watts
96 Leonard Street, London EC2A 4XD

Franklin Watts Australia
Level 17/207 Kent Street, Sydney NSW 2000

Series editor: Sarah Peutrill, Art director: Jonathan Hair, Designer: Ian
Thompson, Picture researcher: Diana Morris, Consultant: Rasamandala Das,
ISKCON Educational Services

Picture credits: Fabrice Bettex/Alamy: 11t. Dinodia: 6,19b, 20, 21t, 21b, 22,
23t, 27t. Gapper/World Religions Picture Library: 14, 26. Kapoor/World
Religions Picture Library: 7t, 11b, 25t, 27b. John & Lisa Merrill: 13t.
Osborne/World Religions Picture Library: 17. Helene Rogers/Ark Religion: 3,
15t, 15b, 18, 19t, 24t, 25b. Topfoto: front cover t. Viesti Associates/Ark
Religion: 7b.

Published in the United States by Smart Apple Media
2140 Howard Drive West, North Mankato, Minnesota 56003

Library of Congress Cataloging-In-Publication Data

Powell, Jillian.
Divali / by Jillian Powell.
p. cm. — (Why is this festival special?)
Reprint. Originally published: London : Franklin Watts, 2005.
ISBN-13 : 978-1-58340-946-6
1. Divali—Juvenile literature. 2. Hindus—Social life and customs—Juvenile
literature. I. Title.

BL1239.82.D58P68 2006
294.5'36—dc22   2005051618

9 8 7 6 5 4 3 2 1

Contents

A happy festival

Divali is a Hindu festival that is celebrated in October or November.

Hindus are people who follow a religion called Hinduism. They believe that God lives everywhere as Brahman, the "Supreme" or "Spirit." They worship him through different deities. A deity is a form of god or a particular god or goddess. At Divali, Hindus remember stories about Rama, Lakshmi, and Kali.

" Divali is one of my favorite festivals. We always see lots of aunts and uncles. "

Satish, age 9

Divali is a happy time when Hindus enjoy being together as a family and giving each other gifts.

Divali is also a festival of light.

Many Hindus celebrate Divali as the start of their new year. It can also be a time for giving thanks for the harvest.

A young boy lights up the dark night with a sparkler at Divali.

Divali is celebrated by Hindus around the world. In India, the festival lasts for five days. Animals are important in celebrations in Nepal, where the festival is called Tiher.

Sikhs and Jains have their own festivals at Divali.

In Nepal, dogs and cows have their own special days at Tiher. They are dressed with flowers and ribbons and given treats to eat.

The story of Rama

At Divali, many Hindus remember the story of Rama and Sita. This is told in the Ramayana, one of the most important Hindu stories.

Rama and Sita's story

Long ago, Rama was a prince, but his stepmother did not want him to be the king when his father died. Rama was sent to live in a forest with his wife, Sita.

One day, Sita was kidnapped by Ravana, an evil, 10-headed king. Rama asked Hanuman, a monkey warrior, to help him rescue Sita. There was a huge battle, and Rama killed Ravana. Rama and Sita returned to their kingdom, and Rama was crowned the king.

These are murtis (sacred statues) of Rama (above) and Hanuman. Hindus keep such images in their family shrines.

At Divali, Hindus celebrate Rama's return.

Some Hindus worship other deities at Divali. Some remember Kali, the goddess of strength.

The festival is also a time for remembering Lakshmi, the goddess of wealth and luck.

Lord Ganesh, the elephant-headed god, the symbol of wisdom, is also worshiped in most Hindu homes at Divali.

> **"** *My favorite god is Ganesh. He looks like an elephant.* **"**
> *Ashok, age 10*

A murti of Sita.

A murti of the Hindu god Ganesh.

9

Festival of light

Divali is a festival of light.

Divali means "row of lights." It may also be spelled "deepavali," "diwali," or "deepvali." At Divali, Hindus put rows of candles and lamps called divas in the doors and windows of their homes. Sometimes they hang twinkle lights around the windows, too.

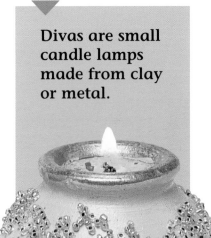

Divas are small candle lamps made from clay or metal.

The lamps welcome Lakshmi into people's homes. Some people also put them there to welcome their dead relatives. They believe that relatives come to visit their family when there is a new moon at Divali.

" On Divali evenings, we turn off all the electric lights so we just have candles and lanterns. It feels really special. "
Sunita, age 10

The streets in towns and cities are lit up with twinkle lights hanging from shops and temples.

HAPPY DIVALI

In India, Hindus float divas across the River Ganges. They say that if a lamp floats all the way across, it will bring good luck.

A diva is set afloat on the River Ganges.

11

Getting ready for Divali

Everyone is busy in the weeks before Divali.

Hindus send each other cards wishing "Happy Divali."

These Divali cards are decorated with pictures of divas.

Families like to clean and decorate their homes so they look their best for the festival. They decorate the rooms with banners, paper chains, tinsel, and flowers, and set out lamps and twinkle lights.

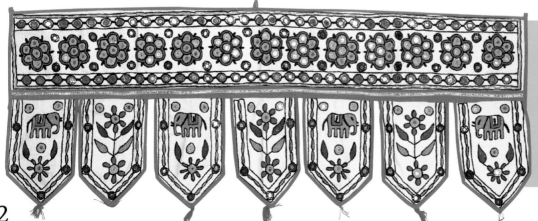

This banner is decorated with tiny mirrors that reflect the light.

Everyone wants to welcome the deities into their home, so they sweep and wash the doorstep. They might also hang garlands of mango leaves and marigolds from the front door.

This woman in Nepal is hanging marigolds from her door to celebrate Divali.

Flower designs are popular rangoli patterns.

Hindus also decorate the doorsteps of their houses and temples with rangoli to bring good luck. Rangoli are patterns made from colored rice or rice flour, paints, sand, paper, or flowers.

" Mom and I once made a rangoli with powder paints in the garden, but the rain ruined it. "
Sangita, age 9

13

Dressing for Divali

Hindus like to look and feel their best for Divali.

On festival days, they take a bath or shower in the early morning and rub their skin and hair with sweet-smelling herbs and oils.

Women and girls often decorate their hands and feet with pretty patterns of henna called mehndi.

Mehndi patterns are traditional for festivals such as Divali and other special occasions such as weddings.

Many people like to buy new clothes to wear for the celebrations, and families often give each other clothes as presents for Divali. In many parts of India, it is traditional for brothers to give their sisters new saris, and sisters to give their brothers new shirts.

▶ A mother and daughter dressed in new clothes for Divali.

▶ A girl wearing a headdress, earrings, and necklaces for a Divali party.

" At Divali, I dress up in a blouse and a ghagra, which is a long skirt with a pretty pattern on it. "
Heena, age 9

Divali is a time for celebrating wealth, so some women also buy new jewelry to wear for the festival.

15

Prayers for Divali

Prayer is an important part of Divali.

Most Hindu homes have a shrine or prayer room, so the family can pray together in front of murtis and pictures of their deities. At Divali, families pray in the morning and evening. They offer God gifts of water, fruit and flowers, rice, sweets, spices, or money.

> " We have a shrine in our living room. My sister and I help to decorate it for Divali. "
>
> Sita, age 9

Hindus repeat the deities' names as they call on them for their blessings.

Many Hindus visit a temple to say their prayers at Divali. Priests wash the murtis with milk and dress them with brightly colored clothes, jewelry, and flowers. Often, there are people singing and playing music.

At Divali in Bengal and other eastern parts of India, people pray to the goddess Kali and decorate murtis of Kali. At the end of the festival, they take the murtis to a river to wash them.

In the temple, Hindus leave gifts of food or flowers for the deities.

Luck and money

Divali is the start of a new year.

Businesspeople try to pay all of their bills before the start of a new year. They take their account books to the temple to be blessed and thank Lakshmi, the goddess of wealth and good luck, for helping them earn money. They send gifts and candy to the people they work with and try to settle any quarrels!

Businessmen asking Lakshmi to bring them good fortune in their businesses during the next year.

Children are often given gifts of money by their grandparents and other relatives.

Families ask Lakshmi to come into their homes and bless them with luck and money. Children may help put out sweet foods and gifts for Lakshmi in front of the family shrine.

The goddess Lakshmi is shown here with a pot of money at her feet.

"At Divali, I paint little footprints with powder paints on the stairs to show Lakshmi the way to our prayer room."

Sunita, age 10

Divali is also a time for winning money! Hindus invite family and friends over to play cards, as they believe Lakshmi will bring them luck at Divali.

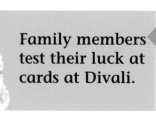

Family members test their luck at cards at Divali.

Markets and bazaars

Divali is a busy time, as families go shopping to buy food and gifts for relatives and friends.

Divali markets and bazaars are decorated with lights, lanterns, flowers, and golden streamers. There are stalls selling fireworks, cards, gifts, and food such as dried fruit, nuts, and candy. Many stalls and shops offer shoppers special bargains at Divali.

A market in India is decorated with colored lights for Divali.

> **"**At Divali, Dad takes us to the market to buy sparklers and fireworks.**"**
>
> Sanjeev, age 9

Some bazaars have entertainment, including camel and elephant rides, and there are loud-speakers playing music for dancing.

Acrobats entertain the crowds at a fair in India.

Actors dress in colorful costumes to act out scenes from the Ramayana, which tells the story of Rama and Sita.

There may also be plays, puppet shows, and parades, acting out events from the story of Rama and Sita.

Festive food

Divali is a time for feasting with family and friends.

Sharing food is an important part of life for Hindus.

Women prepare snacks to offer to family and friends who come to visit.

" Mom is always busy cooking at Divali. I help her. "
Sangita, age 9

Snacks, such as crispy *poppadums* (top) and *samosas* (bottom), are popular.

At Divali, Hindus enjoy festive meals with their family.

Children may have special treats such as sweets, in the shape of divas, made from fudge, coconut, almonds, or chocolate.

At Divali, Hindus eat special dishes of rice and lots of sweet puddings made from milk, sugar, dried fruit, and nuts.

When people are visiting, they take gifts of sweets, dried fruit, or nuts.

Dishes set out for Divali with nuts (right) and sweets (above).

Festive fun

At temples and other public places, Hindus celebrate with fireworks and dancing.

Fireworks light up the night sky, with big public displays in towns and cities.

Many people also buy their own firecrackers and sparklers for parties in their yards and gardens.

" At nine o'clock, after a big meal, we go to watch the fireworks. The firecrackers are so loud they make you jump. "

Ashok, age 10

Divali is also a time for dancing. People get together to do traditional dances such as dandia raas.

Many dances tell the stories of the Hindu gods in mime.

In dandia raas, the dancers each hold a stick and knock it against their partner's stick as the music gets faster.

In some countries, there are street carnivals with Divali queens and princesses. People play music and light lanterns and candles to welcome Lakshmi and other deities.

Giant divas decorate a float at a Divali parade.

Sikh and Jain Divali

Sikhs and Jains also celebrate Divali.

The Sikh festival lasts for three days. Sikhs remember the time when their leader, the Sixth Guru, was set free from prison. People lit divas to welcome him home.

At Divali, Sikhs go to their temple to pray. Later, they celebrate with firework displays.

At the temple, everyone lights a candle and takes gifts of sweets to share.

The Golden Temple of Amritsar is the holiest place of worship for Sikhs.

For Jains, Divali is the start of a new year. Jains remember when their teacher, Lord Mahariva, learned knowledge and wisdom.

The Jain festival lasts for three days. People light their homes with lanterns and candles and share sweets with family and friends. Some Jains fast (go without food) for part of the Divali festival.

A cow dressed with flowers and bells with a crowd celebrating Jain Divali.

Glossary

account books books that record the amount of money paid into and out of a business over a year.

bazaar a market selling all sorts of different goods.

carnival a big street party with a parade of people, animals, or floats.

deity a god or goddess, or an image of one.

diva a small oil lamp made from clay or metal.

guru a leader and teacher of the Hindu, Sikh, or Buddhist religion.

henna a red dye made from a plant.

mehndi patterns painted in henna on the hands or feet.

mime acting out stories or drama with movements rather than words.

murti means "form." The image of a deity used in worship.

parade a group of people, animals, or vehicles moving along together.

poppadum a type of very thin crispy bread.

rangoli patterns made on the ground with colored rice, paints, or other materials.

samosa a fried, crispy turnover with meat or vegetables inside.

sari a type of dress worn by many Hindu women.

shrine a place of worship.

temple a building used for worship and religious ceremonies.

Religions in this book

Hinduism

Hinduism started in India and is the world's third-largest religion, with around 900 million followers around the world. People who follow Hinduism are called Hindus.

Hindus believe in one God, who lives everywhere and in everything as Brahman ("spirit" or "the universal soul"). They worship Him through many different deities, including Rama, Krishna, Shiva, and Durga.

Most Hindu homes have a prayer room or shrine with murtis and pictures of the gods. Families worship the gods by repeating their names and offering them gifts such as water, fruit, and flowers. They also go to mandirs (temples) to worship.

Hindus believe in reincarnation: that we (the eternal soul) live many lives, and that we will have a good or bad life depending on how we lived our past life.

Sikhism

Sikhism is another important world religion from India. There are around 20 million Sikhs in the world. Most live in the Punjab region of India and Pakistan. Sikhs follow the teachings of Guru Nanak (1469–1539) and the nine gurus who followed him. They believe in one God and pray to Him at home and at places of worship called gurdwaras. Their holy book is called the Guru Granth Sahib.

Like Hindus and Jains, Sikhs believe that we live many lives. The most important practices of Sikhism are:
• to keep God in heart and mind at all times
• to live honestly and work hard
• to be generous to those in need
• to serve others

Jainism

Jainism is a religion from India. There are around six to seven million Jains in the world, more than half of them living in India. Jains do not believe in a God or gods in the way that many other religions do. They believe that all living things, including plants and animals, contain a soul, so it is important to love and respect them.

Jains follow the teachings of their great teachers, called the tirthankaras. The last tirthankara was Lord Mahariva (599–527 B.C.).

Index